D1237487

FOLK DANCES OF LATIN AMERICA
WITH CD ACCOMPANIMENT AND EASY TO FOLLOW DANCE GRAPHICS, ORFF AND PERCUSSION ARRANGEMENTS

CONTENTS

ISBN 0-89898-980-9

9 780898 989809

Editor: Debbie Cavalier
Production Coordinator: Diane Laucirica

Dance Graphic Diagram Key

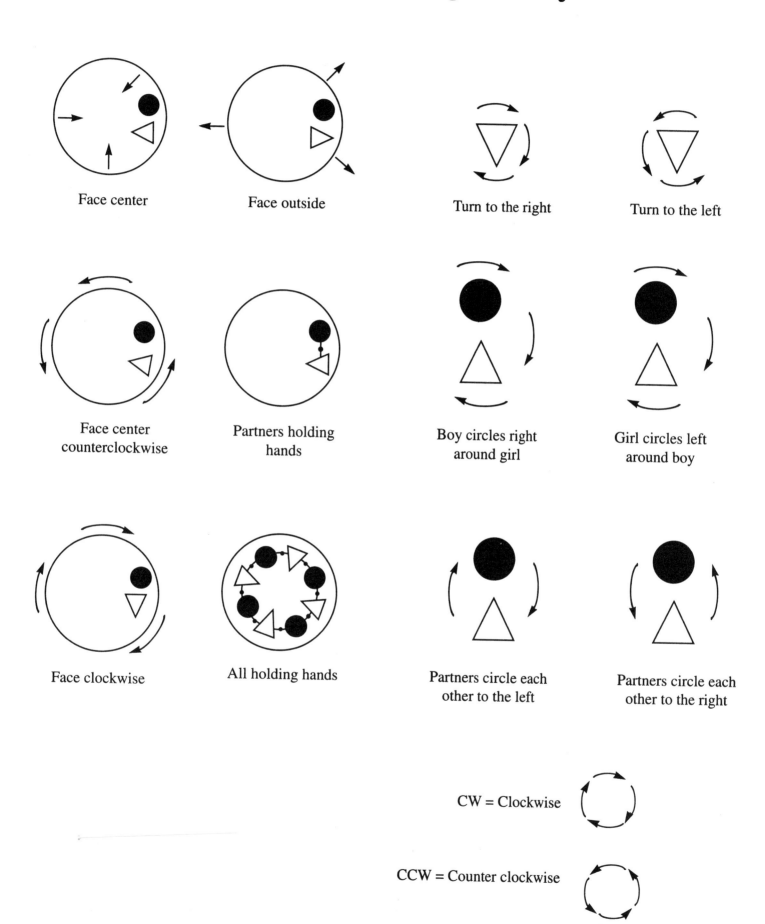

Face center

Face outside

Turn to the right

Turn to the left

Face center
counterclockwise

Partners holding
hands

Boy circles right
around girl

Girl circles left
around boy

Face clockwise

All holding hands

Partners circle each
other to the left

Partners circle each
other to the right

CW = Clockwise

CCW = Counter clockwise

1. Huyano (Peru)

Formation: Single circle, partners side by side, each holding a bright-colored scarf, one end in each hand. All stand motionless facing center of circle with heads bowed during 4 measure introduction.

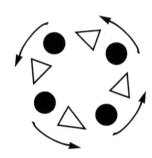

PART 1

4 measures
    Make 1/4 turn to right to face CCW.**
    Take 4 steps forward and 4 steps backward (R, L, R, L and R, L, R, L) raising head and scarf slowly as in prayer.

8 counts
    Repeat (R, L, R, L and R, L, R, L).

4 measures
    Face center. Take 4 steps to center and 4 steps back, raising and lowering scarf. (R, L, R, L and R, L, R, L).

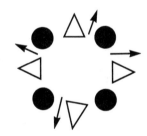

4 measures
    Face outside of circle (turning right), take 4 steps forward and 4 steps backward. (R, L, R, L and R, L, R, L).

PART 2

4 measures
    All face CCW (turn left)
    Count 1: Rock forward on right foot.
    Count 2: Rock backward on left foot.
    Count 3: Rock forward on right foot.
    Count 4: Bring left foot up to right and tap.
    Repeat above step 7 more times, alternating starting foot.
    On 8th time turn in place to face CW.*
4 measures
    Repeat all of above steps (of Part 2) facing CW.

 Boy

* CW - clockwise
** CCW - counter clockwise

 Girl

PART 3

Partners face. Each girl holds end of scarf in right hand and end of partner's scarf in left hand.

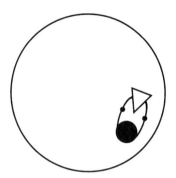

4 measures

Move CCW with partner, using the same step as in Part 2. (One girl will be moving backward as partner follows her). On 8th step, partner reverses direction.

4 measures

Repeat all of Part 3, moving in a CW direction, partners facing. (Boys will be moving backward as partner follows him.)

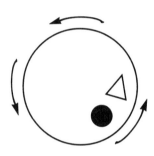

PART 4 (ENDING)

4 measures

All turn CCW and take 4 steps forward and 4 steps backward (R, L, R, L and R, L, R, L).

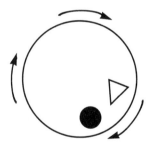

4 measures

All turn CW and take 4 steps forward and 4 steps backward (R, L, R, L and R, L, R, L).

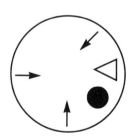

4 measures

All face center and take 4 steps to center and 4 steps back (R, L, R, L and R, L, R, L)
Partners face and place scarves over shoulders and stand with heads bowed.

Note:

On the last 4 measures instead of going out and back, partners face center of circle, place scarves over shoulder and stand with heads bowed.

2. Marinera (Peru)

This dance, one of the most popular in Peru, has been known in the past by other titles. In 1880, a group of Peruvian patriots changed its name to MARINERA, in honor of the loyal "marineros" (sailors and marines) of Peru. It is performed in 3/4 time.

The dance suggests the graceful, rolling, rocking, and turning motions of a ship, and the uneven gait of a sailor on a slanting deck. The movements of feet and arms vary in different regions, but the traditional elements are retained. It is a "danza de pañuelos" (scarf dance), and rhythmic waving of bright kerchiefs is characteristic.

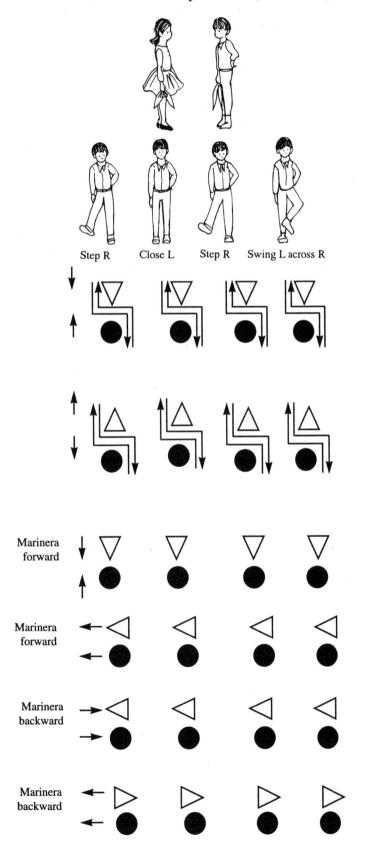

Formation: 2 lines about 10 feet (or less) apart, partners facing. Girls all in one line, arms at sides. Boys all in the other line, with right arm down and left hand in pocket or behind back, palm out. All hold red kerchiefs, grasped in center with ends hanging down.

MARINERA STEP: Step right; close left foot to right; hold. Step right; swing left foot across right; hold. Start next step with left foot.

Introduction: 3 chords. Straighten lines and bow to partner.

PART 1A

2 measures

4 walking steps forward (R, L, R, L), partners passing right shoulders nod and exchange places.

2 quick stamps to right, making 1/2 turn with each stamp, to end facing away from partner.

PART 1B

2 measures

4 walking steps backward (R, L, R, L) partners passing right shoulders nod and exchange places.

2 quick stamps to right, making 1/2 turn with each stamp, to end facing partner as in beginning formation.

PART 2A

4 measures

Take 2 Marinera Steps forward, beginning on right foot. (See above.)

4 measures

Face left and do 2 Marinera Steps forward, starting with right foot.

PART 2B

4 measures

2 Marinera Steps backward, as above, starting with right foot.

4 measures

Face right. Do one Marinera Step backward. Turn left with 5 stamps starting with left foot. End facing partner in original position.

Count 1

Count 2

Count 3

Count 1

Count 2

Count 3

REPEAT PART 1A

REPEAT PART 1B

End with lines 3 feet apart.

PART 3

8 measures

8 rocking steps (in place).
Count 1: Rock sideward onto right foot.
Count 2: Swing left foot across right, point at, and lightly touch partner's toe.
Count 3: Brush left foot backward.
Begin successive steps with alternate foot.
(During rocking steps boys wave kerchiefs at knee level; girls hold diagonal kerchief corners and wave them overhead.)

PART 4A

7 measures

7 heel-toe steps, leaning right. (Make 2 complete turns using these steps.)
Count 1: Step right, leaning to the right.
Count 2: Put left heel forward.
Count 3: Shift weight to left toe.
Repeat, beginning each step on right foot, gradually making the 2 complete turns.

PART 4B

1 measure

2 quick stamps (R, L) facing partner in original position.

PART 5

Repeat entire dance.

PART 5B

Repeat entire dance, omitting Part 4B (the stamps).
Instead: Boys kneel; girls pose with kerchiefs held high.

3. Los Viejitos (Mexico)

This dance represents old men, bent over with rheumatism, who dance, leaning on crooked canes and describe crosses on the ground with their feet.

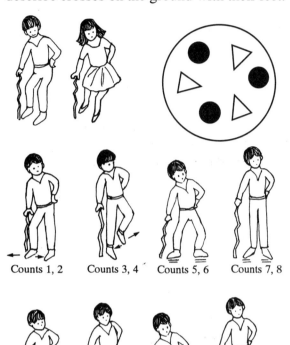

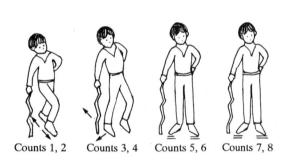

Counts 1, 2   Counts 3, 4   Counts 5, 6   Counts 7, 8

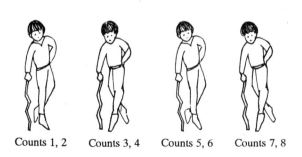

Counts 1, 2   Counts 3, 4   Counts 5, 6   Counts 7, 8

Counts 1, 2   Counts 3, 4   Counts 5, 6   Counts 7, 8

Formation: Partners stand side by side, facing forward. Each leans forward, with the palm of the left hand held behind the left hip, fingers downward. The right hand leans on a crooked cane.

Introduction: 4 beats. Take formation to the cane taps.

PART 1A

8 counts

Counts 1, 2: Stamp right foot to the side, close right foot to left.
Counts 3, 4: Stamp left foot to side; close left foot to right.
Counts 5, 6: Stamp right foot to side; stamp left foot to other side so feet are astride.
Counts 7, 8: Jump, bringing feet together; hold.

8 counts

Repeat.

PART 1B

8 counts

Counts 1, 2: Jump with right foot forward; jump with left foot forward.
Counts 3, 4: Jump with right foot forward; jump with left foot forward.
Counts 5, 6: Stamp right foot to side and left foot to other side so feet are astride.
Counts 7, 8: Jump, bringing feet together; hold.

ENDING 1

8 counts

Repeat Part 1A, once only.

PART 2A

8 counts

Counts 1, 2: Stamp right foot forward; stamp right foot backward.
Counts 3, 4: Stamp right foot to side; stamp right foot to back.
Counts 5, 6: Stamp in place — right, left.
Counts 7, 8: Stamp in place — right, left.

8 counts

Repeat Part 2A.

PART 2B

8 counts

Counts 1, 2: Leap sideward to right, placing left toe behind right heel; pause.
Counts 3, 4: Leap sideward to left, placing right toe behind left heel; pause.
Counts 5, 6: Leap sideward to right, placing left toe behind right heel; pause.
Counts 7, 8: Leap sideward to left, placing right toe behind left heel; pause.

8 counts

Repeat Part 2B.

ENDING 2 (1st time only)

8 counts

Repeat Part 1A, once only.

Count 1   Count 2   Count 3   Count 4

Counts 5, 6   Counts 7, 8

Counts 1, 2   Counts 3, 4   Counts 5, 6

Counts 1, 2   Counts 3, 4   Counts 5, 6   Counts 7, 8

Counts 1, 2   Counts 3, 4   Counts 5, 6

PART 3A

8 counts

> Counts 1, 2, 3, 4: Slowly turn head; right, left, right, front.
> Counts 5, 6: Stamp right foot to side; stamp left foot to other side, so feet are astride.
> Counts 7, 8: Jump, bringing feet together; hold.

8 counts

> Repeat Part 3A.

PART 3B

8 counts

> Counts 1, 2, 3, 4: Turn 1/4 right; walk slowly R, L, R, L, leaning on cane, toe in, dragging feet.
> Counts 5, 6: Stamp right foot to side; stamp left foot to other side.
> Counts 7, 8: Jump, bringing feet together; hold.

8 counts

> Repeat Part 3B.

PART 4

32 counts

> Repeat Parts 3A and 3B, as above.

ENDING 3 (1st time only)

6 counts

> Counts 1, 2: Stamp right, left in place.
> Counts 3, 4: Stamp right foot to side; stamp left foot to other side so feet are astride.
> Counts 5, 6: Jump, bringing feet together; hold.

5 counts

> Repeat Ending 3, omitting hold.

5 counts

> Repeat Ending 3, omitting hold.

PART 5

7 counts

> 1/4 turn; stamp right, stamp left, leaning on cane.
> 1/4 left turn (facing front); hold.
> 1/4 turn; stamp right, stamp left, leaning on cane.
> 1/4 right turn, facing front and hold.

PART 6

8 counts

> Counts 1, 2: Slowly bend knees, dipping down.
> Counts 3, 4: Slowly straighten.
> Counts 5, 6: Stamp right foot to side; left foot to other side.
> Counts 7, 8: Jump, bringing feet together.

8 counts

> Repeat above.

ENDING 4 (1st and 3rd times only)

5 counts

> Counts 1, 2: Stamp right, stamp left in place.
> Counts 3, 4: Stamp right foot to right side, left foot to left side.
> Counts 5, 6: Jump, bringing feet together.

PART 7

REPEAT ENTIRE DANCE FROM BEGINNING, OMITTING ALL ENDINGS.

ENDING 5

Repeat Ending 4.

4. SI, SEÑOR (Brazil)

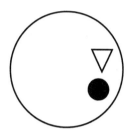

Formation: Boys facing partners in CCW position; girls facing boys in CW position. Boys left shoulder and girls right shoulder to center.

Introduction - 3 chords

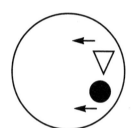

Measure 1
   Boys starting with left foot, girls with right.
   Take 3 sliding steps toward center (step, close, step, hold).

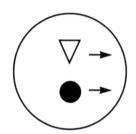

Measure 2
   Boys starting with right foot, girls with left.
   Repeat, moving to outside of circle.

Measures 3, 4
   Repeat measures 1 and 2.

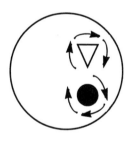

Measures 5, 6
   With same steps (step, close, step, hold) make complete turn to the right.

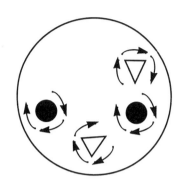

Measures 7 - 12
   Repeat measures 1 through 6.

Measures 13, 14
   With same steps (step, close, step, hold) beginning with right foot, turn from partner, snapping fingers, and nod to neighbor, turn back to partner and nod.

Measures 15, 16
   Repeat, beginning with left foot.

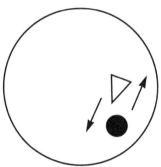

Measure 17, 18
move to new partner

Measures 17, 18
   With same steps, pass partner to right and meet new partner. Without stopping, repeat dance from the beginning. The dance is repeated 4 more times, with the solo instrument alternating from marimba to flute and back.

5. Palapala (Argentina)

The Gaucho, or Argentine "cowboy" wears a "poncho," which is a large square of material with a hole cut in the middle to put his head through. While on horseback this protects both the Gaucho and his horse from the weather, rain or shine. It can be as elaborate as desired with fringe, etc. This dance is performed in 2/4 time.

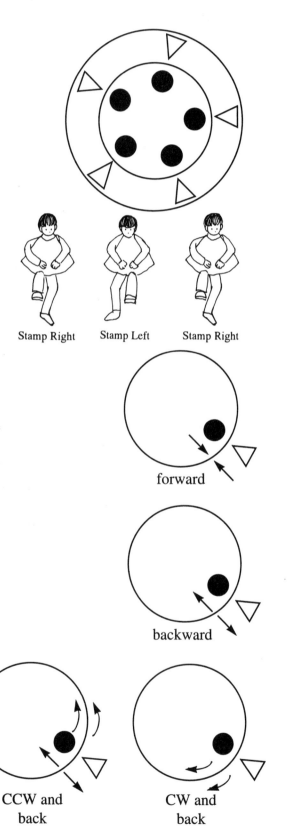

Stamp Right   Stamp Left   Stamp Right

forward

backward

CCW and back   CW and back

Formation: Boys, wearing ponchos, form an inside circle facing out; girls form an outside circle facing in. Circles a short distance apart.

Step: The basic step is done very quickly in this dance: stamp, stamp, stamp, hold. (R, L, R).

Introduction - 3 chords

PART 1

Measures 1, 2

Hold closed fists in front of chest with elbows out to sides, raise and lower elbows so that arms fly like a buzzard in time to music; meanwhile each starting with the left foot, take 3 steps to each measures moving forward, accenting each beat with a stamp. (Stamp left, stamp right, stamp left, hold and stamp right, stamp left, stamp right, hold.)

Measures 3, 4

Same as above, taking three steps backward, then three more steps backward, to place.

Measures 5 - 8

Same motion, taking the three steps CCW and back and then CW and back.
Repeat Part 1 two more times.

PART 2

8 measures

Saw like a carpenter, while balancing from side to side keeping time with the feet to the stamp, stamp, stamp, hold steps.

Repeat Part 1 two more times.

PART 3

8 measures

Pound like a shoemaker, balancing from side to side using the basic step.

(Stamp, stamp, stamp, hold.)

Repeat Part 3.

Repeat Part 1 two more times.

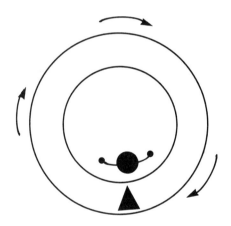

Girls circle sideways

PART 4

8 measures

Boys hold arms outstretched in front of them, doing basic step in place, while girls, holding out their skirts wide so as to touch the next girl, circle around sideways to the left with basic step. Repeat dance doing each part ONE TIME ONLY, from Part 1 through Part 4 with no repeats. At ending each boy brings down his outstretched arms, catching whichever girl is in front of him, enclosing her in his poncho.

6. El Llanero (Venezuela)

This couple dance might be called the national dance of Venezuela. It is danced in the parks during carnival time. The use of maracas to accent the rhythm adds interest and authenticity to the dance.
This dance is played in 3/4 time.

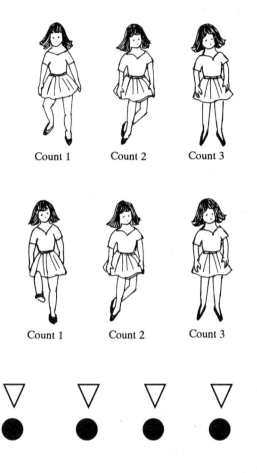

Count 1   Count 2   Count 3

Count 1   Count 2   Count 3

Step: Stamp Waltz

sideward
   Stamp sideward with right (Count 1).
   Step in back of right with left (Count 2).
   Step on right in place (Count 3).
   Repeat, beginning on left foot.

forward
   Same as above, stepping forward with right (Count 1).
   Step in back of right with left on Count 2.
   Step in place with right (Count 3),
   making rocking motion.

Formation: 2 lines, couples facing: Boy's hand on hip, girl holding skirt.

Note: Front foot is left for boy, right for girl. Rear foot is right for boy, left for girl.

Introduction: 3 guitar strums

PART 1

Measures 1 - 4
   Dance 4 "stamp waltz" steps in place, beginning with front foot.

Measures 5 - 8
   Forward and back with 4 "stamp waltz" steps in place, beginning with front foot.

Measures 9 - 16
   Repeat all of above.

Measures 17 - 24
   Repeat measures 1- 8 again.

Count 1   Count 2   Count 3

Count 1   Count 2   Count 3

PART 2

Measures 1 - 8

Circle away from partner with 7 forward "stamp waltz" steps, beginning with front foot, finishing with 2 stamp, in place, holding for count of 3. (Each person makes a complete circle in place, ending with stamps facing partners.)

Measures 9 - 16

Repeat.

PART 3

Measures 1 - 8

Partners travelling toward rear of room.
Stamp sideward with rear foot (Count 1).
Brush front foot forward (Count 2).
Stamp across rear foot with front foot (Count 3).
Repeat above step 7 times.

Measures 9 - 16

Repeat from beginning of Part 3, but this time travelling to front of room and beginning with front foot.

PART 4

Measures 1 - 2

Step sideward with rear foot (Count 1).
Brush front foot forward (Count 2).
With knee raised and toe pointed downward, cross foot over in front of rear foot (Count 3).
Repeat above, alternating feet.

Measures 3 - 8

Repeat all of Part 4, finishing by turning away from partner with 3 stamps and a bow to partner.

REPEAT ENTIRE DANCE.

7. Tamborito (Panama)

During this dance, the performers are encircled by spectators, who clap (twice to a measure), sing, and call out complimentary remarks to the girls, who are dressed very beautifully in "polleras." The girls show off their costumes, while the boys try to out-do each other with their quick squatting steps, showing off to both girls and spectators. Dancers are accompanied by drummers seated in the center, who beat out varied rhythmic patterns in 2/4 time. Originally, the only accompaniment was solo and chorus singing, drums and clapping. When stringed instruments were added, the dance was called "Tambor de Cuerda." A violin, flute, clarinet, guitar, and marimba are chiefly heard in this version.

Step Right   Close   Step Right

Count 1   Count 2

NOTE: Units in this dance are identified by different main instruments used to repeat the same short tune.

Introduction: Face and get ready to 3 guitar chords.

Formation: A single circle facing CW, boys standing behind girl partners. Girls hold wide skirts high in both hands; boys keep left hands behind their backs and manipulate straw hats with their right hands.

Step: Starting with right foot: Step, close, step (R, L, R).

VIOLIN TUNE 1

8 measures
Dance 8 quick two-steps (see above) around the circle.
Count 1: Step forward on right foot; and bring left up to right.
Count 2: Step forward on right foot.
Hold. Alternate.

VIOLIN TUNE 2

8 measures
Repeat as in Violin Tune 1.

FLUTE TUNE 1

4 measures
Face center; step forward on right foot, slowly bending knees and trunk. Bend again and straighten slowly, replacing right foot.

FLUTE TUNE 2

8 measures
Repeat Flute Tune 1.

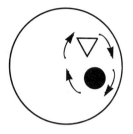

VIOLIN TUNE 3

8 measures

First circle left around partner with 8 two-steps, starting with right foot. Boys: Three two-steps in place starting with right foot, followed by 1 squat-step (crouch with left leg extended, then right leg, bending forward at waist).

Boys repeat 3 two-steps and 1 squat-step.

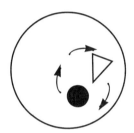

VIOLIN TUNE 4

8 measures

All face center; move left starting left foot, 8 draw-steps.
Count 1: Step sideward with left foot.
Count 2: Bring right foot to left.
Repeat to make a total of 8 steps.

CLARINET TUNE 1

8 measures

Boys circle right around girls starting with left foot doing 8 two-steps while girls do 8 two-steps in place starting with right foot.

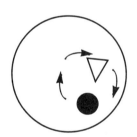

CLARINET TUNE 2

8 measures

Girls move left in small circle starting right foot, doing 8 two-steps dipping skirts. Boys follow partners through the two-steps with right foot.

VIOLIN TUNE 1 THROUGH CLARINET TUNE 2

Repeat entire dance as above.

VIOLIN TUNE 1 AND 2

16 measures

Repeat as above. End facing partners.

8. Fado Blanquita (Portugal/Brazil)

A popular dance of Portugal in 2/4 time. Danced by people of Portugese extraction in Brazil.

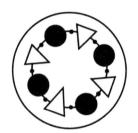

Steps: Walk, schottische, stamp-swing.

Formation: Couples in single circle, facing center, all hands joined.

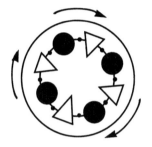 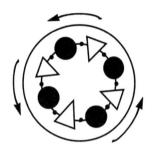

PART 1

Measures 1 - 8
   Run 16 steps CW, beginning with left foot.
   Repeat CCW.

Measures 9 - 16
   Repeat above CCW.

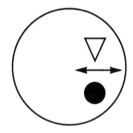

Sway R,L,R,L

INTERLUDE
Measures 17-18
   Partners facing; sway slightly to right, left, right, left.

PART 2

Measures 19 - 21
   Partners hook right elbows. 3 schottische steps turning around to place, beginning with right foot (step-step-step-hop).

Measures 22 - 24
   Repeat, joining left elbow with neighbor.

Measures 13 - 18
   Repeat Part 2.

Sway R,L,R,L

Measures 25 - 26

Face center; sway right, left, right, left. Boys' hands on hips, girls' hands on skirt.

PART 3

Measure 27

Step to right, swing left foot across right; step left, swing right foot across left.

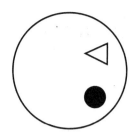

Jump half turn
facing outward

Measure 28

Jump in place making a half turn so that you are facing out.

Measures 23 - 24

Repeat Part 3 facing outward. Finish facing center.

PART 4

Measures 29 - 36

Repeat Part 3.

Repeat Parts 3 and 4.

REPEAT ENTIRE DANCE. (Only 1st half or Part 1)

Repeat half of Part 1.

Repeat Part 3 and 4.

Repeat half of Part 1

Orff and Percussion Arrangements
by Debbie Cavalier and Sandy Feldstein

ABOUT THE INSTRUMENT PARTS

The indicated intruments have characteristic sounds. Other instruments
within the same basic sound families may be added or substituted.

For example:

Maracas - Cabasa, Chocallo, other shakers

Tambourine - Hand Drum, Jingle Sticks, various shakers

Claves - Tone Block, Rhythm Sticks, Wood Block

Drums (high, low) - Bongos, Hand Drum & Conga Drum, 2 Pitched Conga Drums

Cowbell - Triangle (do not allow to ring)

Castanets - Woodblock, Spoons

Guiro - Cabasa, Tambourine

LATIN AMERICAN FOLK DANCES
1. HUYANA

2. MARINERA

3. LOS VIEJITOS

4. SI SEÑOR*

*Repeat in key of F, then transpose to C, F, C, F.

BMR05115

22

5. PALAPALA*

*Play three times, then transpose patterns to keys of G, C, D.
BMR05115

6. EL LLANERO

7. TAMBORITO*

*Repeat in the key of F (four times) then transpose to G (twice) and B♭ (twice). Repeat the entire form from from the beginning and end in the key of F.

8. FADO BLANQUITA

BMR05115